The book is in three parts.

Your child's teacher will tell you when to start a new part.

Each part can be used for a whole term.
The activities can be done in any order.
Some activities can be done several times.

Please help your child fill in the date when they finish an activity.

I did this activity on ___Tuesday 19th Nov.___

There are more activities for Green Level in the Copymasters and Games Pack.
Your child's teacher may send some of these home, too.

PART 1

There are eight activities in Part 1.

They will help you to practise:

- counting to 100, forwards and backwards.
- spelling numbers to 100.
- adding and taking away with numbers up to 50.
- using money.
- multiplying and dividing by 2, 3 and 4.

Do each activity as often as you want to.

One hundred

Can you find any packets or boxes that say they have 100 things in them?

100 Baking Cases

Cotton Wool Balls

Contents: 100

100 PIECE PUZZLE

ALIEN PIRATES!

Draw the packs here:

If you can, count the things and see if there are one hundred!

I did this activity on _____

Make ten £10 notes and find 10 buttons, pasta wheels or counters to be £1 coins.

Take turns with a partner.

I'll give you some money.

Write down how much it is in figures and in words.

£37
thirty-seven pound

Check your spelling on the list at the top of page 7.

one	six	twenty	seventy
two	seven	thirty	eighty
three	eight	forty	ninety
four	nine	fifty	one hundred
five	ten	sixty	pounds!

Try questions like this, too:

How much more to make £100?

£70
seventy pounds

I did this activity on

-------------------------------   -------------------------------

You need three 10p coins and twenty 1p coins.

Do each sum with the coins.

 I spent 22p and 19p. How much altogether? _____

 I spent 11p, 25p and 10p. How much altogether? _____

 I spent 17p and 17p. How much altogether? _____

 I spent 15p, 16p and 7p. How much altogether? _____

Work with a partner.

Make up sums for each other.

Use coins to help you.
Write some of your sums here.

I spent [ ] and [ ]

Total: _____

I spent [ ] and [ ]

Total: _____

I spent [ ] and [ ]

Total: _____

I spent [ ] and [ ]

Total: _____

I spent [ ] and [ ]

Total: _____

I spent [ ] and [ ]

Total: _____

I did these pages on _____

Tables square

Draw the missing counters and complete the sums.

2 × 3 ⟶ = _6_

3 × 3 ⟶ = ____

4 × 3 ⟶ = ____

5 × 3 ⟶ = ____

Put the 3 times tables facts on the tables square:

×	0	1	2	3	4	5
0	0	0	0	0	0	0
1	0	1	2	3	4	5
2	0	2	4		8	10
3	0	3				
4	0	4	8		16	20
5	0	5	10		20	25

Use playing cards to practise your tables.
You will need:

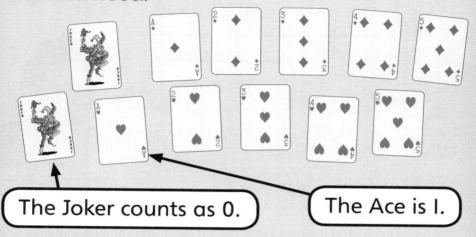

The Joker counts as 0.

The Ace is 1.

- Shuffle the cards. Put them in a pile.
- Take two cards at a time.

- Multiply the numbers together.

4 lots of 5.
5 + 5 + 5 + 5

4 × 5 = 20

- Check on your tables square!

I did this activity on

---------------------------------   ---------------------------------

You need twenty 1p coins.

We are sharing money.

Half each!

What is half of 18p? _____

What is half of 14p? _____

You can't always share things exactly!

Half of 7p is 3p each...

...and 1p left over.

What is half of...

8p? _____   9p? _____

10p? _____   11p? _____

12p? _____   13p? _____

I finished this page on _____

Apples
20p each

Bananas
25p each

Crisps
23p a bag

Raisins
15p a box

How much change
from 50p? _____

How much change
from 50p? _____

How much change
from 50p? _____

How much change
from 50p? _____

How much change
from 50p? _____

I finished this page on _____

Marbles

You need a piece of card
and five marbles.
Make an arch or a tunnel:

 1  Fold your card
in half.

2 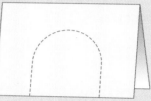 **3**

Cut out an archway.

Or fold your card in three:

and make a tunnel.

Score four points for each marble
you get through the arch (or tunnel).

If you haven't got any marbles,
you can roll coins.

I got three marbles through the arch.

Twelve points!

I got sixteen points!

How many marbles
did I get through? _____

I did this activity on

------------------------------   ------------------------------

Take two cards

Make 18 cards like this:

| 1 | 2 | 3 | 4 | 5 | 6 | 7 | 8 | 9 |

| 1 | 2 | 3 | 4 | 5 | 6 | 7 | 8 | 9 |

(or you could use playing cards).

Work with a partner.
Shuffle the cards. Put them in a pile.

Take two cards.
Make the biggest number you can.
5 6 or 6 5 ?

65!

Then your partner does the same.

41.

The person with the bigger number wins all four cards.
Take turns to go first.

Here's another game.

Shuffle the cards. Put them in a pile.

Take two cards. **5** **3**

You must count backwards from that number, until you get to the number that is 10 less.

53, 52, 51, 50, 49, 48, 47, 46, 45, 44, 43.

Your partner will check. You win the cards if you get it right.

Take turns at this.

I did these activities on

-------------------------------   -------------------------------

-------------------------------   -------------------------------

PART 2

There are eight activities in Part 2.

They will help you to practise:

- counting to 110.
- adding and taking away with numbers up to 55.
- learning number facts off by heart.
- using money.
- multiplying and dividing by 2.

Do each activity as often as you want to.

And you can still do any from Part 1!

Secret numbers

Find our secret numbers.
Use the number line.

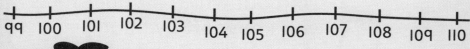

99 100 101 102 103 104 105 106 107 108 109 110

My number is bigger
than one hundred.
It is smaller than one
hundred and two.

It is _____.

My number is bigger
than one hundred
and four.
It is smaller than one
hundred and six.

It is _____.

Ask someone to take turns with you.
Choose a number on the number line.
Give your partner clues to find it!

I finished this page on _____

Off by heart

Find out which number facts you know off by heart.

That means you don't have to work out the sums.
You just <u>know</u> them.

Try these.

1 + 1 = ____	1 + 3 = ____
4 + 3 = ____	2 + 4 = ____
2 + 0 = ____	3 + 0 = ____
2 + 3 = ____	4 + 1 = ____
0 + 4 = ____	1 + 2 = ____
2 + 2 = ____	3 + 3 = ____

Check

 Highlight any you know off by heart.

20

Now try these.

$4 - 1 =$ _____ $1 - 0 =$ _____

$3 - 2 =$ _____ $2 - 2 =$ _____

$5 - 5 =$ _____ $4 - 3 =$ _____

$4 - 0 =$ _____ $5 - 3 =$ _____

$5 - 2 =$ _____ $4 - 2 =$ _____

$2 - 1 =$ _____ $5 - 4 =$ _____

Choose a fact you don't know off by heart.

$3 + 5$ ⟶ 8

Write it on a piece of card …   with the answer on the back.

Practise until you know it.

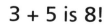

$3 + 5$ is 8!

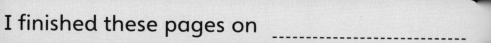

I finished these pages on _____

Seeing patterns

Doing sums on a calculator can help you see patterns.

Do these on a calculator.
If you start to see the pattern, do them in your head.

Then check: ✔ or ✗

50 – 7 = _____	50 – 4 = _____
40 – 7 = _____	40 – 4 = _____
30 – 7 = _____	30 – 4 = _____
20 – 7 = _____	20 – 4 = _____
10 – 7 = _____	10 – 4 = _____

38 – 30 = _____	29 – 20 = _____
38 – 8 = _____	29 – 9 = _____
42 – 40 = _____	34 – 30 = _____
42 – 2 = _____	34 – 4 = _____

45 + 10 = _____

27 + 10 = _____

36 + 10 = _____

19 + 10 = _____

42 + 10 = _____

24 + 10 = _____

13 + 20 = _____

23 + 20 = _____

33 + 20 = _____

18 + 20 = _____

28 + 20 = _____

38 + 20 = _____

33 − 10 = _____

33 − 11 = _____

33 − 12 = _____

33 − 13 = _____

33 − 14 = _____

46 − 12 = _____

36 − 12 = _____

26 − 12 = _____

47 − 12 = _____

37 − 12 = _____

27 − 12 = _____

I finished these pages on _____

Double your pounds

Double your money

£1   £

£1

A game for 2 people.

£2

- Make ten £10 notes and find 20 buttons (or counters) to be £1 coins.

£10

- You also need a dice and two counters.

- Put your counter on any empty space to start.

Double your money

£2   £

I played this game on

------------------------------   ------------------------------

Double your money

£3

Double your money

£5

£1

- When it is your turn, throw the dice and move that many spaces. Take the amount of money you land on.

- The first person to get £50 is the winner.

£2

Double your money

£10

Double your money

Make this game and play on your own, or with a partner.
You need a piece of card a bit bigger than this book.

1

Cut off two little squares.

2 Fold along three sides.

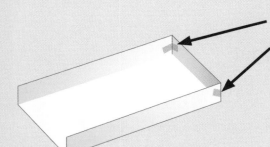

Put sticky tape on the corners.

Or you <u>could</u> cut up a cereal packet, to make your game.

3 Draw on numbers like this:

Use a pound coin to play the game.

Play the game!
You can roll your
pound three times.
Add up your score.

If your pound
lands like this,
decide which
space it is
<u>mostly</u> in.

I get 8!

I played this game on

-------------------------------   -------------------------------

Hidden pennies

You need ten 1p coins and a partner.

Put the pennies on the table.

Then hide some with your hand.

How many pennies are hidden?

Seven!

Take turns at this.
Try again with 12p or 14p.

I did this activity on

-------------------------------   -------------------------------

28

How much money have I got?

24p

How much money have I got?

£1·24

When we write amounts of money, we use £ or p, not both.   ~~£1·24p~~

Ask your partner to give you some money in coins.

Count it up. (Your partner can help you.)
Write down how much it is. Do this six times.

_____   _____   _____

_____   _____   _____

I did this activity on _____

Counting on

I can take away by 'counting on'.

$12 - 9$

Here are 12 counters:

I can take away 9:

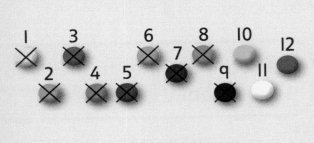

Count on from 9:

10 11 12

$12 - 9 = 3$

That's 3.

Do these by counting on.

$14 - 11 =$ ____

$18 - 16 =$ ____

$24 - 19 =$ ____

$40 - 38 =$ ____

$17 - 12 =$ ____

$32 - 28 =$ ____

You can count on with money, too.

26p - 22p

23   25
  24   26

22p

4p

26 − 22 = _____

22 + _____ = 26

Do these. Use coins if you want to.

36p − 31p = _____   43p − 38p = _____

19p − 12p = _____   11p − 8p = _____

50p − 44p = _____   27p − 20p = _____

25p − 19p = _____   33p − 29p = _____

I finished these pages on _____

PART 3

There are nine activities in Part 3.

They will help you to practise:

- counting to 120.
- adding and taking away with numbers to 60.
- multiplying and dividing by 2, 3, 4 and 5.
- telling the time.

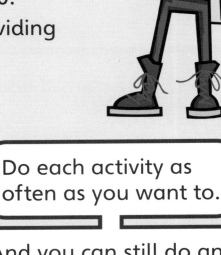

Do each activity as often as you want to.

And you can still do any from Part 1 or Part 2!

Number quiz

Ask someone these questions.

Can they get ten out of ten?

The answers are in **red**.

1. How many days in a fortnight? **14**
2. How many eggs in half a dozen? **6**
3. How many minutes in an hour? **60**
4. How many letters in 'Wednesday'? **9**
5. How do you spell 40? **forty**
6. How many days in April? **30**
7. Is 43 an odd number? **yes**
8. What is a special name for 100 years? **century**
9. How do you spell 80? **eighty**
10. What is 10 add 20 add 30 add 40? **100**

I did this activity on

------------------------------   --------------------------------

I can make number patterns with my calculator.

When I press

5 **+** **5** **=** **=** **=** **=**

I get 10, 15, 20, 25.

It counts up in fives.

Try this on your calculator.
If it works, try these too:

2 **+** **2** **=** **=** **=** **=** **=** ....

4 **0** **–** **2** **=** **=** **=** **=** **=** ....

1 **0** **0** **–** **5** **=** **=** **=** **=** ....

Say the numbers out loud
to help you learn the pattern.

1 **2** **0** **–** **1** **0** **=** **=** **=** ....

Say what number will come next, <u>before</u> you press = each time.

5 0 − 1 = = = = = ...

5 0 − 2 = = = = = ...

5 0 + 5 = = = = = ...

5 + 1 0 = = = = ...

Write the next four numbers.

23, 33, 43, _____, _____, _____, _____

99, 89, 79, _____, _____, _____, _____

59, 58, 57, _____, _____, _____, _____

I finished these pages on _____

35

Fill in the missing numbers.

0, 4, 8, 12, ____, ____, 24, ____, 32, 36

____ × 4 = 16   ____ × 4 = 20

7 × 4 = ____   0 × 4 = ____

3 × ____ = 12   10 × 4 = ____

28 ÷ 4 = ____   8 ÷ 4 = ____

12 ÷ 4 = ____   36 ÷ 4 = ____

____ × 4 = 4   ____ × 4 = 8

____ × 4 = 24   4 × 6 = ____

4 × 8 = ____   9 × 4 = ____

I finished this page on _____

Quiz yourself!
Check that you know your
5 times table facts.

8 × 5 = _____   0 × 5 = _____   5 × 9 = _____

2 × 5 = _____   5 × 3 = _____   4 × 5 = _____

5 × 5 = _____   6 × 5 = _____   5 × 7 = _____

5 × 10 = _____

Check

How many fives make....

45? _____   15? _____   5? _____

50? _____   25? _____   40? _____

10? _____   35? _____   20? _____

I finished this page on _____

Sixty pence

You need four 10p coins and twenty 1p coins.

Put the coins in a bowl.

Take a handful of coins.
Count them.

Take another handful.
Count them.

Write down what you get.
Add the amounts together.

$$23p + 18p = 41p$$

Do this six times – or more!

_____   _____

_____   _____

_____   _____

Use the coins to help you do these:

54p – 19p = _____   43p – 21p = _____

31p – 24p = _____   59p – 39p = _____

$$\begin{array}{r} 31p \\ + 18p \\ \hline \end{array}$$ $$\begin{array}{r} 36p \\ + 24p \\ \hline \end{array}$$ $$\begin{array}{r} 17p \\ + 17p \\ \hline \end{array}$$

26p + 19p = _____   26p + 29p = _____

26p + 16p = _____   26p + 26p = _____

$$\begin{array}{r} 46p \\ - 27p \\ \hline \end{array}$$ $$\begin{array}{r} 59p \\ - 19p \\ \hline \end{array}$$ $$\begin{array}{r} 60p \\ - 43p \\ \hline \end{array}$$

I finished these pages on _____

Use playing cards to practise sums in your head.

You don't need the picture cards.

Take four cards.

Remember! You can add in <u>any</u> order.

I'll add them like this:

 + +

5 add 5 is 10, add 7 add 1 makes 18.

Ask a partner to check your adding.

Ask your partner to make up puzzles for you, like this.

Take four cards.
Don't let me see them.
Add them up.

Tell me what they add up to.
Show me three of them.

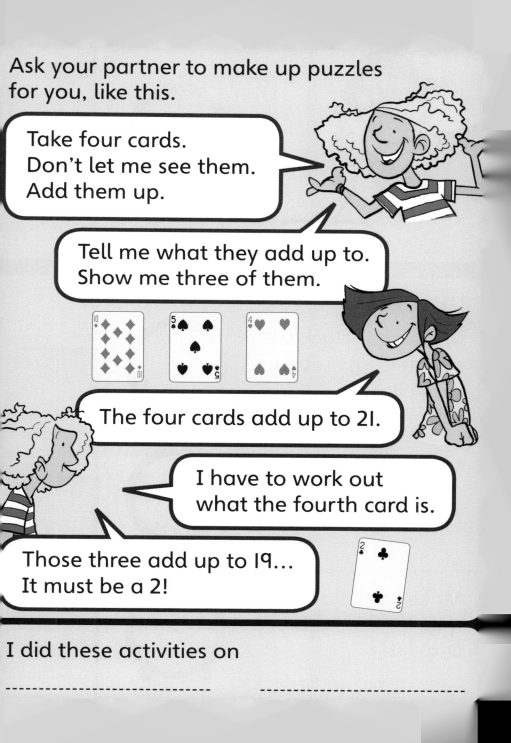

The four cards add up to 21.

I have to work out what the fourth card is.

Those three add up to 19...
It must be a 2!

I did these activities on

-------------------------------   -------------------------------

It's seven o'clock.

Use a real clock with hands.

Make your clock show quarter past seven. Draw it.

Make your clock show half past seven. Draw it.

Make your clock show quarter to eight. Draw it.

Practise telling the time.
Use a clock with hands.
Start at one o'clock.

Ask someone to turn the hands,
a quarter of an hour at a time.

Say what the time is.

Try other times
if you want to.

If you want to,
ask your partner
to make up questions
like this:

7:45

How many minutes
until eight o'clock?

I finished these pages on _____

2 pencils in a pack.
How many pencils in:

2 packs? _____

5 packs? _____

8 packs? _____

10 packs? _____

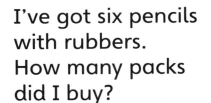

I've got six pencils
with rubbers.
How many packs
did I buy?

 6 ÷ 2 = _____

_____ packs.

How many packs for:

8 pencils? _____ packs

18 pencils? _____ packs

14 pencils? _____ packs

12 pencils? _____ packs

3 animal pencils
in a pack.

How many pencils in:

3 packs? _____

9 packs? _____

5 packs? _____

4 packs? _____

I've got six animal pencils.
How many packs did I buy?

6 ÷ 3 = _____

How many packs for:

30 pencils? _____ packs

21 pencils? _____ packs

12 pencils? _____ packs

24 pencils? _____ packs

I finished these pages on ------------------------------

Match the clocks

What is the time? Which clock shows the same time?

_____

_____

_____

I finished this page on ----------------------------------